I0186924

NEW AMERICAN WRITING 43

(2025)

NEW AMERICAN WRITING

Edited by Paul Hoover at 369 Molino Avenue, Mill Valley, CA 94941, and published in the August of each year. The submission period is limited to September through January. We do not consider email submissions or submissions lacking a self-addressed stamped envelope.

Published by MadHat Press, PO Box 422, Cheshire, MA 01225, in conjunction with OINK! Press, 369 Molino Avenue, Mill Valley, CA 94941.

Copies of current and recent issues may be ordered at madhat press.com.

A three issue subscription is $36. Single issues: $15. Copies mailed to Canada: $22 CAN. Elsewhere outside the country: $24. All back issues except No. 4 are in print and available for sale. Send a check directly to *New American Writing*, 369 Molino Avenue, Mill Valley, CA 94941.

To order back issues online, go to newamericanwriting.com. There is a link on that website that connects with the editor's email address, viridian@hotmail.com. Please indicate issues you wish to order. We no longer accept orders made through CCNow of Minneapolis.

Copyright © 2025 by *New American Writing*.   ISSN: 0893-7842
                                                 ISBN: 978-1-968422-07-3

Cover photo by Paul Hoover
Cover and page design: Marc Vincenz

New American Writing is indexed by Index of American Periodical Verse, Humanities International Complete, and Annual Index to Poetry in Periodicals.

Distributed by Media Solutions, 9632 Madison Boulevard, Madison, AL 35758.

Printed in the U.S.A.

NEW AMERICAN WRITING

CONTENTS

NEW AMERICAN WRITING

DENISE NEWMAN

Dictator School

Who made the garden where the made people are kicked out? Who made the out to go into? Blame's relationship to the ancient *blaspheme* explains everything. Adam saying "She did it" made of Eve a wanton thing. *Thing* is slang for vagina in Greek, relating to German *Ding*, followed by Dong; make a game of pinning it on the other and teach it to the children. Believing my ass and the donkey's ass are not the same is like saying my as is self-made, is like Samson bragging: "With the jawbone of a donkey, heaps upon heaps, with the jawbone of an ass, I have slain a thousand men!"

Set

It is what it is, he ways. Pain or pleasure? Hidden in the Ethan Allen bedroom set—is what to women, humiliation? How about bringing it out under the trees so the walnut husks can rain down on the colonial-style bed, bureau of mace and nation, bureau of lace and glorification. It is Ethan Allen of the Green Mountain Boys (why *boys?*)—cruelty and intimidation. Follow the grain to make a rip cut. Is war *what it is* and so every body by design is fucked, or *what?*

Important Things

After mass, he introduces himself: "I'm not a man, I'm a wolf, he ways and the priest extends his hand, Nice to meet you, I'm the King's vagina." "Maybe you can interpret my dream." The priest nods and fetches a warm washcloth. As the wolf wipes its face, he sees someone watching from the back of the church and motions to her: "Come closer, we're doing important things here." The watcher is moved to say, "I'm done being normal."

Important things does not mean you wake from a dream and its institutions stop existing: important things is not necessarily about waking or even befriending a wolf. The watcher, once cast as Red, realizes what she took for normal was someone else's fairy tale, like Vladimir telling Estragon, "I'll do Lucky, you do Pozzo.... Say, 'Say, 'think Pig?'"

for Hendl Mirra

Brief and unlasting

—Brief and unlasting like the iris' flag unfolded, enthralling
        with rain-scent and mutable violet, or the seeming violent-
in-swiftness that builds when the fertilized egg divides—zygote,
        morula, to blastula—the berry-shape becoming hollow in divisional
detail, as when a star begins to form, the dense molecular cloud
        congealing within nebula. Through telescopes we've glimpsed
their creation towers, ladders reaching through green fire, climbing
        toward a farther light.—Or solar flares, their massive coronal eruptions,
this beauty in creation and destruction. So too in language when
        Homer describes Meriones' arrowpoint piercing Adamas' groin
till he falls: "And the black blood flowed and the ground was wet with it."
        Or in Bosnia, the Dutch soldier fleeing with an infant during
the genocide, the barbed and feathering seconds streaming at once. So too in
        April, the fire asleep in each tree but summoning us with green.

Gap

The sudden space between us and him, the boy dressed in camo, waving
a semi-automatic weapon, spraying bullets into the holiday crowd,
wounding several before being tackled by a half-costumed Santa, but
    right before
the gap closed between us, the pistol he waved became knife, the mall just
    a clump
of trees on the prairie where we were settlers, then the knife became a stone
in the hand of someone having taken unrightful claim to a cave,
overlay after overlay tumbling back, centuries, but I swear when the five
    wounded
fell, those baubles—on the Christmas tree by the fountain—dropped and
    became
apples, soft mealy apples, and people stared at them, their faces lit
with a blush-red like those bystanders outside in the parking lot's strobing
    lights
where a thick frost fell and continues to fall like snow, deep as it is fine.

G.C. WALDREP

Yellowhammer

I want's metanoia

amid the fields
of brute endeavor

we will
all be conquerors

intuition
of the dark in-
between, a seed

the breath
presses
to the cold heart

midnight regard
for October's
burnt lute

lute I burned
(as in some myth)

tonic memory
suiting up

its everywhere

its perpetual
soul-
ward reclamation

The Disappearance of Song Pierced
by the Found Measure of Good Friday

The train, heard but rarely seen, is hauling toxic waste
away from neighborhoods to our north, bearing it south.
When I hear it I think about the brilliant forests
I once walked through. The mind, a bee in search
of its right hive. What sweetness it has found!
Lead halo of my house in the coarse decalogue of want,
I lay my ashes down in the unseen days, a bruise
occulted in moonlight's hotel. The other animals
dip their heads at me, raise their paws in some salutation.
I prefer the oxygen hospice with its blue-white detailing,
its filled-in pool. Wide artery of the clouds ablaze,
what new nothing remains for me to inhabit (as though
dwelling were a plundered psalm). The wedding
in Smyrna I never attended, show me the photos
if you can—limit of my natural impresencing. I curl
inside my kneeling, I make a fist of beauty, a crowded
altar. It's dawn on the third day of my *vita nova*
in the hostel of surgeries, where persuasion lingered.
A shadow is not a veil, insist various ancient authorities,
& I believe them, I double-check my calculations.
My tongue is a rainwater carnival against which
a spade is leaning. I peer through its prism,
wanting the new refraction. It recognizes the animals
when it meets them, rarely & most often in pieces
torn from other pieces. This isn't a dream but
an intervention among other interventions. It's not rare,
it's not even mourning in the disused chapel (or
not a *proper* mourning). Penance, where the dead gather
away from the shreds of what their affections
all but possessed. How they catch in the chain-link.
I drive across the ice to where the planet touches
the *more* of the heart's window, which opens & closes.
My father, in his petty pension of not-dead-yet,

his left hand absentmindedly stroking the stray cat
my mother has named after a movie star from their youths.
Twinned urns of capitalism from which a new silence
breaks, I abjure your false declensions, the spurious
Latin they weigh & rend. Bee-mind of the hive at rest
in December's lucid bone, narrow as a grave being
overwritten by sleep's miracle-cure: send me
the words night parries, let me wake to them, flayed
shadows I crawl inside, some resurrection-in-waiting.
Solace grazing at the site of the hemorrhage,
a shining quartz displayed in the hospital museum—
I can see it now, I've done the math of obsolescence,
I stumble past the new fields of solar panels
flashing in winter's asymptote of sun. Allegory
is cheap. Ghosts are imaginary. Here, where the witness
guides the thread through the needle's compound eye
in full view of judge & jury, I resolve to happen
twice. Make this my court report, my Judas-testimony,
a purgation of sorts, a kenosis. I empty myself
of the ache of nowhere accumulating inside this song.

Prevenience

forehead of the deer
against which
the wind strums

zodiac of the need-be

revolving
in the nectar's shine

dwelling in the milk

of right action
(that spry flame,
oxygen's
partisan entreaty)

prayer house
of the dream's page
turning

as a shade in space

a single
dark lake, audible
at certain frequencies

the deer watching
from the glory of their
principled embrace

wintry field
set off from the fire
tower by a mist

access patent
of dwelling-life
by the well's lash
lifting (a reprieve)

the gift of hospitality
bearing away

adjunct Jerusalems

a wind
the ash reaches
by way of the mark

perspective suffers

why then dwelling
as descent

(among angles)

(their bluish-white
gothic
scathing the page)

which is the forest
of *begin again*

at macadam's edge

the chronic
hotel of voice
slipping

beneath the solstice

ALEXANDRIA PEARY

Here's to Tomorrow
Northampton, Paris, Berlin, Rome, Tokyo 1997–2022

Near a penciled-in building, CAFE UMLAUT, near a billiard green
wall, a few [color] blocks away.
  In a "balance of graphic and depicted," the citizenry are 195 flags and
20 pennants.

Conversing in mottos, state and national, at an outdoor café, they
order vintage pastry. Futuristic espresso & a "confectionary palette with
whimsical calligraphy" to enjoy with sonnets, with ghazal.
  At the table of contents, a drawn-in chair, ♥ ♥ ♥ 4 across, 5 down, we
make strategic moves. Under a rebus of clouds.

———————————

Lift this stanza w/ a finger or pen cap. Jim and Dara drive past in a
golden Pulitzer car, Shahid in a window at La Fiorentina with the Beloved.
Emily Dickinson leans over the tree line with watering can.
  An alley is added ♣ when a passage is crossed out in a used paperback
of Steinbeck, G. Stein, Simic's "Stone."
  The waitress is reading on break (sandpaper sound of chair taken from
the bar) SHAKE BEF REFRI AFTER OP

Side streets of Terry Eagleton vis-à-vis Kristeva, D. T. Suzuki, Sebald &
Walter Kempowski, her recent customers. A can for cigarette butts,
  industrial-sized can of Amalfi tomatoes.
  Vesuvius is in the Berkshires, Mt. Fuji has moved to the Rockies,
Kilimanjaro is on the
  Appalachian trail: Everything is possible again.

Poetic Victory Vase

wrap-around sentence of people at a café
@ an outdoor café   a people sentence,
depicted on an espresso cup*

gold plated iambic pentameter on the rim
ceramic city block, geometric storefronts
"A woman is walking a poodle that's 1/2 a word

... heads around the corner. A dapper waiter
w/ tray of pastries from 1950s Italian cinema
approaches the cut & paste table where a customer

sips   melodious espresso,
spoons clink in ice cream, reddish wine."

Another lap. The poodle on her skirt un- / ravels
At the next drive by, wrap-around, pencil, mini.
Men w/ wasp waists, kohl eyes & red clay legs

replace the waitstaff. There are sticker ants
because of a pastry fallen on the sidewalk
in a peel-off line of poetry   é   &&&&
          Nightingale of an ˜ is up next.

near the handle] Beauty is tru
Adding sweetener to unheard melodies
John, doesn't that urn depict rape? -rights of citiz   rig of wo

What mad pursuit? What struggle to escape?
          ~~stack of battle horses~~

---

* cup is on a table circled in another poem

At the next drive by, mini, pencil, wrap-around, suit
near cursor angels, handles
on this poetic victory vase.

OLGA MASLOVA

The Book of Hours

If I sit on this bench long enough,
I turn into the sound of dusk
spilling over the trail's border:
the swoop of peregrine falcon,
dragonfly drone, hot, dripping
breath of a passing dog,
its owner's uneven steps,
the tides of crickets' a cappella
tumbling at the porch door
of October.

Dyes bleeding
from the day's garments
caught in the lashes:
the yellow ochre
of the goldenrods
and thistles'
faded purple—

colors of stained-glass couple,
Maximilian and Mary, Duchess
of Burgundy in the Basilica in Bruges,
sunlit, alive, in love for
five hundred forty years.

When Mary died,
her Book of Hours
bereaved Maximilian
embellished with twining thistles.

The bumblebee is stirring
in thistle's purple heart

behind the shutters
of the illuminated *A*.

In the Basilica's gift shop,
I bought the print of Mary and her falcon
on the ill-fated hunt, chased
by three black skeletons. You bought
an earlier flight through Dallas.

In Bruges now it's almost autumn;
still summer here: the water in the river
warm, rolling over
my breasts and thighs.
I wrap my knees around the current,
my old familiar lover:
I will be back next year,
next Lyeto, Лето,
the Russian word for "summer."

Splash in the dark,
the heron gliding,
or is it Charon
steering his boat
over the Lethe?

Will there be
next summer?

Whichever
comes first:
your Birthday
on the twelfth of twelfth,
Russian roulette
of flu complications,

or canceled Airbnb in Paris
still sending the reminders
to both of our emails.

Talking To the Gone

                    kind of day
They come more and more often
                    these days

                    The gone—
they go more and more often
                    into the gone place

                    All is left
practice my conversational skills
                    build vocabulary

                    build courage
to follow their faint tracks
                    on dry creek beds

                    built a threshold
low gray weathered split-rail fence
                    I swung over onto

                    October prairie
brimming soundscape: the gone gathered
                    rumbunctious, unruly

                    not waiting for a turn to speak:
unsmiling black-eyed woman, her hoarse whisper
                    susurrates the maple leaves

                    the river under bluffs
splashing, rippling, chortling *chastushki*
                    old Russian folk songs. Dad?

Birch branches bounce
under the waltzing magpie. It's you. My darling,
you were always a terrific dancer

Geese writing in the sky
a list: born—check, lived—check
gone—check, check, check

ANGIE ESTES

What the Night Is Thinking

A hidden spark of
darkness flashed: that's how,
the Kabbalah says, the universe
began—like the moment when
I wake each morning to the eternal
jukebox of my brain: *night and you and blue*
Hawaii: the night is heavenly and you
are heaven to me, Elvis sings.

In the beginning *was*—

                  but how can the beginning have
a past? The world was created,
according to the Kabbalah, by pronouncing
letters and numbers—and some cicadas,
it's true, do appear only where they were
13 or 17 years ago, something like
pages in a manuscript, before and after,
verso and recto, although
pages of course can be,
like the sky, either inscribed
or blank. As I drift

               back to sleep, Kathy Young and the Innocents
keep singing *a thousand stars in the sky*
make me realize
that if *dreams come true*
in blue Hawaii—why are the stars
winking at me, and why
are there no family photos
of feet? The only ones I've seen
are on my birth certificate: two miniature

bear paws patting off, black tracking
white, from where the beginning was.

The Very Lastness of Things,

Inframince, was perhaps the word Lacan went out
to the waiting room and whispered

into his patient's ear: a barely perceptible
thinness that Marcel Duchamp said cannot be
defined: the warmth rising

from a seat just left, the whistling sound
made by walking in velvet trousers,
the reflection from a window

or mirror: it could be
the movement of your final breath
through air, the waft of your perfume

from the sheets when I make my bed
the next morning: Hopkins' I caught this morning
morning's minion like the weight of nectar sipped

by the hummingbird from a bouquet beneath
the tent at Millie's funeral or the calligraphy
of fireflies slicing commas into

the night: the sound of your silk slip
sliding up or the last slip of the last
iceberg floating in the sea.

CAPTCHA

There will be silence before
it begins: soot black, lamp black

in Japan, one writes with gray ink
instead of black for a funeral or when
writing condolences, which indicates
that the death was sudden: you didn't have time
to completely prepare
the ink or say
goodbye: *You couldn't*
talk to him on days he was
painting clouds

What I love is when
the cardinal dives full speed
into the window, flops
to the ground, and a few minutes
later opens
one eye, spreads a wing as if
opening a hand dealt
at poker, and flies into

some afterlife: A man in North Carolina buys
used guns from pawn shops and melts
down the barrels in order to transform
things that exist that take other things
out of existence: he says you can
get 1100 King James Versions of
the Bible out of the barrel
of a single Remington rifle: Run

your finger down the black sutures
of my notebook's spine: then wake to
the ultraviolet light of sunrise
on a Dreamliner: on slides
from the electron microscope
place arrows that point to
mitochondria: touch...move arrow
closer/ don't touch...move arrow
away: touch don't touch

SUPRITHA RAJAN

from *Mosaic*

Stone 154:

→ a pointed, directionless
seeing, a noticing freed
from watching, from looking →
liquid movement of eye
settling without precipitate, what
moves → through brevity
and never condenses to
the briefly noted → occurrence
recurring without cause, the sum
of what fails to accrue → few
and far between, fruit not fit
for ripening, that sits and stews

*

→ not collecting and bundling
thoughts, but letting them
go, sift and fall → bits of snow or sleet
dissolving into → a mental scrapbook
soaked through and → through → duration
without object, light receding further
into light → then all of a sudden → right on
cue → loosened seed of strawberry
on the tip of the tongue → a reminder
or remainder of something tart, out of
season → its eat by date past due

*

→ it indicates a mood, what happens
happens → happened → following
a marked trail bedded with pine needles →

→ a plotted, plodding hike → up
then down → place to untense, un-
think, forget the list of "to dos" →
draw a blank to which nothing
sticks → free to float, dry up or fall →
reduced to a hue with no particular
point of view → crown of branches
framing sky → sky framing
bare branches and not a single cloud
pasted to it → a turn → turning →
without progress, without transition →
standing in the lull between arrive
and arrived → *shit where am I* →
POSTED note stapled to a tree putting
trespassers and hunters on notice → sign
no one has to see or read → to exist

Stone 209:

If I should never make an appearance, if
I emerge, but emerge only as green would
in a field of grass, if like a bud reared
in a forest of cold winds, no light should ever sail
my petals, no bird sip nectar from my blooming face,
if I should never feel rain on me an indiscriminate
affection that distinguishes me as a singular existing thing
apart, how will you ever find me, and if found,
how will you know to gather all those bits and pieces
lying on the ground that could belong only to me?
Or will you lie down inside my disappearance
like you would lie down on a field of grass
so my body becomes yours, and I could belong to you,
to your gaze as it scans the sky for stars?
Or will we meet, as mist meets a face, when you turn
to the folded page of a book and touch
the field of open spaces where your eye and hand
hold all the love and grief that was once mine
and, long buried, can still be heard whistling
through blades of grass to sound your ear?

MADINA TUHBATULLINA

Light as Plastic

I.

The wispy ends of morning
lie on the immaculate balcony. The windows
throw the nets back at God, try to make us visible.

In perpetuity, a name is a child's tantrum,
fights to manage the wanting.
I inspect it in the light and put it on a drying rope.

A secret hides in the holes of chipped-off paint,
we've built a labyrinth to see it slowly.

II.

I cannot grow bigger than my doorframe.

I am called to touch a vase that glows purple
and sticks to fingertips with its flatness. That's how I keep you here
to tell you I want to be liquid, and how
we never understood serpents.

Back on the balcony, I am holding a bucket by the rim.

Factory

Our overused words have clogged the air.
We are material.

Something pulls a strand of our hair when we sleep
to jitter our minds into dreams.

A crack in the wallpaper?
I saw it yesterday so I got used to it.
It would be easier for me if you became a planter.

The smoke—every unimagined life,
abandoned babies that were never found.

Hope is a shoulder under a shoulder
a multiple defense against a singularity, but

nothing apart from this Wednesday,
nothing beyond it. Among past people,
we,

transcendent,

delusional,
don't pretend.

PATTABI SESHADRI

Her Knees
after Homer

Belt-lashed to my high seat
on the commuter bus,
the fennel has swallowed the marsh
between the bay and freeway,
killing the other suitors
to her vague attention,
mud, water, goose nest, and grass
without edge.

I cross the threshold
of the apartment.
Everything still smells to me
of licorice and salted strawberries,
along with hints of baseball mitt and hair spray,
and tuberose, yes.
Does she remember me.

I love her knees.
They could be the subject of an epic.
She hates them because they're too big.

They will never be photographed.
Dusky, forensic, animal and mineral,
I like to span them with my hands.
"I kneaded the wax in my strong hands
till it became soft, which it soon did
between the kneading
and the rays of the sun-god."

It's hard to believe that the sun alone
generates all this heat.

But there it is,
the photo negative of emptiness,
and within it we are edgeless.

Corona

The quarantined city sleeps
revealing its true loneliness
The beam of a streetlamp fills with rain
Music echoes from empty bars
The streets lead uphill Into darkness

There are signs of life here and there
The blue glow of a television on a wall
A flower arrangement in a window
A man wrapping a woman in his coat
Mission Dolores
the Mission of the Sorrows
breathes from its pink walls into the night
as it has for 400 years

And so everything seems the same
just a little quieter
It's all online now anyway
so nothing needs to be real
I run my hands down the stucco
of the mission wall,
look a stranger in the eye
Nothing's really there
but I don't know if it ever was
I might have caught the disease
and died long ago

Send My Roots Rain

(presence was broken for a while

(stillness was floating in plaid dark

like a promise to the living and the

dead

*

(and the most horrible heartburn

(and the old couple in the kitchen

(lights out, lights out, waiting for

sound

(and the leaves roll just like faces

(and the faces blow like thieves (and

we all keep our explosions (and you

taste joy in the night

        *

(and the lost boys answer slowly

(and the corpse picks up the phone

(and we all claim that we're holy

(God won't leave our dreams alone

DONNA DE LA PERRIÉRE

Aftermath

they felt ridiculous
at first: the heaving stars, the botched
wings, and the snow
falling hushed and thrall-like over the town

blossoms collect in jaws,
the acrid seas of the horizon, the hospice room
tethered to the heat of the day

outside voices pile up
on the horizon, the sky seared and biblical,
the dry river a collapsed vein

All Souls

rib-gaunt
trees, angled
sky, little

fists, then
fields upon
fields upon

fields: the white
moon brackets
the opening

fallow, the
darkening
seed, the

harrowed
wheel

JAMES SHERRY

Civil Civil Military

From the empire's core,
From the moment when boundaries
All fail from climate's ministrations,
Appeals to wisdom overflow
With excess life.
Denying does not dilute its symptoms
Of heat, of broken value,
of corpse-shaped ash.

Climate catastrophe will be a gesture
Of the earth at the moment of sloughing off
Another excess, another template to simulate
Conditions of rules and rulers,
In speech called human, in another frame partial,
But let's not say wasted construction
Of competition from terrorist
Trees taking up space
And the microbiome, those agents of nutrition,
Of the narcissism of engineers and poets
At the phalanges of alarms ticking down
People think are about them
When it's not identity,
But acts and gestures, a shorthand
For classifying an instant in an instant
Planetary judgment long deferred
By human ambition.

To truncate lengthening time, the gardener prunes
Strict metrics that are simply earthly.
Speech slows down thought
And practice at once and wouldn't manufacture
Similarity to make self seem

One italic gate
To another world we'd wish.

DAVID MUTSCHLECNER

The Metaphysical Hybrid 1

A face drawn in profile

                looks across
                etiolated gray slate

                at a chalky
                heavy smudge

        So this is the cloud
        my closed
        form comes from

and returns to. On the bus home

        on the radio:
        Santana's *Europa*:

                Bitter-sweet pleading —

I can't tell
if it is God's or our's. The guitar's

            bent note
            cuts me
            from the cloud

Though I washed
the slate

I could not bring myself
to erase the face

The Metaphysical Hybrid 2

I don't remember using
a band-aid as bookmark in
The Coherence of Theism

> —a text
> that dissects
> sentences

seeking cogency. My mother

abrades her leg while going through
the lawn chair

> —cries through the blood: *I just*

wanted to see
> *the beautiful birds that go*

across. A few sparse weeks

and the book scabs over
I can no longer

> parse
> nor cipher save

by wounded wonder. *I want*

to see the beautiful birds
> *that go across. Look,*
they wheel
> *and its all the white*

Nomen

Frosted glass
            beneath which
        a moon-lamp casts
    her pearl-
            gray halo. I pause

    while passing
                nearly everyday
            the little window

    through which the light
                recedes
            into a moment closed

            and carried off

                the way a name
            that moves through modes
    of peroration

    is carried off and closeted
                before we know
            or choose to know
    beauty's omen

    whisper-hummed from under
                its umber penumbra

Three for Creeley

1

Word curls into circle
but grows
obscured. World

not sated by
the faux rich groom we offer her
The starving dark

consumes the room
unless by
angelic syntax

we give the world again
her fluent child, hence give
creation back

to herself. I hear
the evening descant:
logos trills with eros, even now

2

Carving the wood
    he comes

        to fixate
            upon the shaved curls

    A would-be
    sea hawk soars

above the waste and wonder, amber
                dust and parings, paper thin
                in the pour of window light. Each curl

could be a bird. Rough and unfinished,
                the terminal flight
                in convergent-opening

3

        Take the image of language as a cone
        with a tip like a child's small open mouth
        above the ever-expanding base. Descending

        through the cone, language grows widely
        and wildly fecund. Words tangle and spawn
        and morph into other words, the lectionary a
        simulacrum of manifold creaturely wonder

        Now ascend the cone. Language lessens
        and yields to silence, as if the top-mouth of
        convergent-opening, holds back
        its word, the single word. The holy

        paradox is that the child's mouth gives birth,
        as in constant cosmogony, to all the volubility
        below, even as she remains quiet

KIT ROBINSON

Chimurenga Rebel
after Thomas Mapfumo

Everything that happens
Happens millions of times
As your time and my time
Are entirely different
Yet one in the same

The line curves with the earth
A coat of many colors
Clinging to a rock
Hurtling through space
The straight line too is circular

The return of the chorus
Anchors us in this space
A groove at one with time
Where we can be together
In the river's flow

Carried along by the current
The current battle for liberation
That is our life on earth
Is framed in the small actions
Of the everyday

A phone call from the beyond
A dream of a tall stranger
Walking alone in a town
Seashells in a coastal road
Distant music

Let the dancers have the floor
They know how to use it
The sky is a tent
A big tent of clouds
To shade the dancers

Este Es Nuestro Changüí
after Changüí de Guantánamo

This road we are going on
Stretches out in advance of our going
Of hills and waters
It is the very knowledgeable guide
We stop only to go hard
Into the starry night
To the lady of our midnight hour
The child of our morning
The man of noon
This road, this road

Skin of our skin
Sliding down the scale
From rich to poor in a day
Abandoned to dreams at night
We move against the times
Absorb the taste of flames
Stoop to enter the door
Sit among revelers
March with the masses
Happy to be with the people

The call of the instruments
Is heard in the air
A joyful sound
From somewhere over there
The neighbor must be sawing
Or turning on the tap
We live in the busy city
The density's over the top

Whenever you get here
We will be glad to see you

TERRY PETTIT

Going North Toward Pine Creek on Route 183 with a Friend

Traveling through the Sandhills in the dark, we crest with every swell and then slide toward a hidden creek. Oncoming headlamps in the distance lift above the ridge, fireflies in the mist, headed toward Kearney or North Platte.

We are going to a small stream hidden beneath watercress in a pasture that stumbles North until it leans into the Niobrara. Rainbow and brook trout live in the cool, timeless water that flows with little attention from ranchers, farmers, and big bluestem. Its sandy banks are fragile and calve like icebergs if a barbed wire fence is disabled and cattle slide into the stream.

Tonight, at the Forgiven River Inn, I dream of becoming a cold-water fish feathering in and out of the bubble stream, rising to feast on a Goldenrod Beatle or perhaps to get a better view of moonlight.

White Privilege

I am not on alert when I bend for water at the fountain.
The church I attend has never been bombed.
I can drive a Mercedes or a Lexus without harm in Alabama.
I wasn't saved by the wisdom of my grandma.
I can lie down in the grass without courage.
At the rest stop I let my dog off the leash.
My children do not press their faces to the glass
as we pass the graveyard.
We can breathe.

DON BERGER

This Is Different

They say that when people get older their hair turns
White and their skin tightens
And it's true. Look at her,
She's more beautiful

Now than ever seen.
And what she's said to us
Forms a new aisle.
She's using more email now,

But still climbs to the window
With her pillow, sighing, minding the quiet.

STELLA WONG

Inference

You offer me an English-language
Qur'an. And thanks

for the toad skin gold
kiwi. Pauses

for the grandfathered milkweed.
Things I don't know include

how to distinguish
between the missing

vowels of the abjad.
The sugar, red

and silver maples'
indents. How to wire

the two lamps after
you leave.

Leak

The lake effect snow
blows in like forgiveness

overnight and warm.
Unearned and yearning—

ending. Otherwise known
as spill or bleed, sound

leakage takes place
when the mic

picks up other sources
when we're too close

or live. Your last words—
sleep well.

KARIN RANDOLPH

Good evening. Hello. Hello hello. So hi I'm ok sorry.

I'm impulsive. Sorry. Sorry sorry sorry. I"m sorry my milk isn't good anymore. I'm sorry I'm eating cake with a plastic fork. I'm disappointed with this plastic fork. You disappoint me. Your optical instruments are disappointments. And now I'm confused about recycling a plastic fork. I call a friend take out the trash call another call my mother. Tie a scarf around my neck to separate my head from my body. Feel density amiably its edges warm against me.

Tomorrow will be partly cloudy with a chance.

I salvage what I can. Go up and down curving bridges. Then it's
Venice. Then it's not. I check under beds. Don't know if the
baby is wailing or keening. It could be a case of mistaken
identity. I watch the day disappear. I get feelings. I don't use
chemicals. I'm trying to cut down. Mourn victims. Search for
evidence. I'm honored and humbled. The birds fidget. Glaciers
return. One ice cube at a time. I clear the refrigerator. Put the
keys in the lockbox.

ALBERT MOBILIO

Breathing Room

There are lives twice as long as others;
they might look back on those
behind them like runners nearing
the finish line relieved
not to have been out of it so early.
We wake one day to an understanding
about our diminishment yet
by evening, we've turned that corner—
the present is everything; its tedium
flaring in the window's reflection.

You get tired of being this way.
Some plans go awry & other plans
are made elsewhere, somewhere
elaborately empty.
Perhaps we are beautiful when we
close the book & draw up
the covers; the means of accumulation
mastered, the complaint undone.
Unheard behind this window, the night sky—
boundless—still roars.

Small Town Theodicy

So much I had to say about the pope & there was
this tiny annihilation going on, underlings
groping pillows in ancient-colored light.
The accuracy of the depicted musculature
impresses tourists, but locals offer only
inherited disappointment: this savior, you hear
around the grotto is all allegory, no nerve.

The toys we bought for the kids likely won't
keep them occupied for long; they'll rip up
the backseat with the usual intemperate oratory,
then tears, more tears, then pitiful guile.
Morning will bring out neighborhood celebrities:
Wisdom Bo's filthy spaniel & Auntie Imogen,
that fairer vision of mothers lost.

Regard the centurion's task—to blow on a spark
till it flames into assurance. Moments ago
I was writing an interpretative essay about
interpreting things, things indistinguishable
from one another, then, without warning,
those very things went quite otherwise & *What
a goddamn world*, I said to no one.

My broad-shouldered brooding hasn't moved
any of the usual needles even though I took that
human potential course & have told everyone
it knocked me right off the milk train.
Who is this priest I've heard is dying to meet me?
Instead of a crucifix, he wears a pinecone
around his neck & affects the manner rustic.

See how they're selling the new intercourse:
lots of holler then a big mope around the throne.
My pope furrows his brow; this isn't a simple job
like rural electrification or Viennese circumcision!
You & you & even you must pull your own
weight, belly up, eyes fixed on the ceiling,
stupid yet alert to mortal intimations.

The scent gone rampant through the camp;
our once sprightly plumage damp with heaven's
oily drip. Where does a man thus disarmed go?
I hold on to senseless fluency because I've eaten
this meal before. Here come so many sins you couldn't
count them & would die if you did, your raw
ape's mouth open to conspiring night.

MOHAMMAD AZARM

Translated by Kaveh Bassiri

Mohammad Azarm is a leading postmodern poet in Iran, working within various formal and conceptual constraints. He was part of a bold generation of Persian writers called the "Poets of the Seventies" (referring to the 1370s in the Iranian calendar, which roughly maps to the 1990s). They rejected established poetic conventions and experimented with language and forms. Azarm is the author of six books of poetry and two books of critical essays.

The poem, "[Put in Quotes]," is from his third book, *Haoma*, the title of which refers to a spiritual plant used by Zoroastrian priests in ceremonies. The poems "Temple" and "Holy of Holies," from *Hayakel* (2016), came out of an experimental project that developed in three stages. First, in 2009, Azarm published online a concrete poem, collaging a visually hard-to-read Persian essay on Derrida with Post-it notes. Next, a series of online comments and exchanges were posted about the concrete poem. Finally, *Hayakel*, a metatextual book, was created from a collage of these exchanges and the original piece. The word *hayakel* is plural for *haykal*, which is referenced in a quote from the Bible that appears at the beginning of the book and means "temple": "Jesus answered and said unto them, 'Destroy this temple, and in three days I will raise it up'" (King James).

[Put in Quotes]

If you get put in quotes, what concession do you make to the day? Would you convey caution with of course or consign it to a special case and proceed to evasion?

The option is out of service until I restore the color of bread to the skin, offer the seat to the snow, and stir the heat with word of mouth into the human-thickening coffee. With perpetration that has not been carried out, it keeps the clouds out of the absolute, reciting them from memory in the language of shadows. Then it is enough for it to tilt the moments, sit smack in the middle of a memory becoming the place for things in disarray, even for the destruction of trifling things. When it nods to the left, its thoughts and trifles tilt right; if it nods to the right, its trifles and thoughts tilt left. Either they become a calendar or a swamp over its head that is neither the limits of must nor indicative of a determination. It is that difficult place where it is stuck even if it is gone. A common thing for a prayer, a trifle for a plea.

Temple

Not to assimilate   in my opinion
The texts we write transform into an oak tree
Outside of heaven   caught in a game of signifiers and subject

To assemble   is ahead of the performance   more of the age
Even if you do something disorderly   even braver, fail in something
And the outside   doesn't present a complete and perfect picture of the
        background
So all of this can become coordinates
Coordinates that can't reach the depth of collage

Perhaps not just the sound   perhaps God's heaven has stopped
No even higher th …   higher than what?

Can one turn Lot's wife, caught inside the people's supplication
In all the seeds   in all the transformations, into a verb?

Information without vision   moves war from this   from …   from this
        totality
To a declaration of a few theories and one other invisible text
A past that chews the future and proceeds

Holy of Holies

And from the frontiers you have stormed into the ears
with the terse technique of a snake's leap.
Thought picks the context from the periphery
to play the role of an orchestra conductor.
From now on
no question may gather war around itself
or put death to use again.
Do you yearn for the already realized terms?
Besides, so many things won't nullify the power of time.
What is important is that you become a frontier to grant the apostles
all these possibilities and doubts that are the seen-most language of the world.
This history is ever so happening.
And the understanding of the go-betweens has exceedified the reach of
life in the fading of language.
Whose hands should be used,
and whose strength restored without ifs and buts?
Tell me what necessity necessitates the world?
What saying of the way of saying would help us carry on without ourselves?
More importance should be placed on all the beliefs and excesses
not on a body that enters a bottle in order to swim.

CINTIA SANTANA

unknown caller

I knew no one in Houston
        but I answered.
I knew the world rent
        but I heard the voice say
patient is the soil,
        the wind shyly coaxing
rye grass into song.
        unshorn, the sheep waits
no less than the sheep berry,
        and four
are the meanings of *ba*.
        may you know
shade grass and shore,
        under day's high shoulder
sure doors.
        eschew the lie
if not the shun;
        shame, a lesion
unlike any other.
        even the fang waits
for its fang lesson.

unknown caller

an ember   at the mercy of winds

       you cannot trust   a blind eye of light

   arced through darkness

       torches   what feeds it   fuel   fed by rain

a grief aglow   roars   swallows whole   mountains

       sentries   of the perennial   palms

       crowns of palms   burning   stars

       along an avenue   govern nothing

willow are we

       and more   so   on a windy santa ana day

   remember   the ember   within

              the fire

   before   the fire   and after

the quiet   once again

       listen   I tell you

the space required   for blooming

can be small   you are still

     alive   the wind   bridles your hair

BRIAN COCHRAN

Reading Mahmoud Darwish During an Eclipse

> *On the roof of neighing, I will cut thirty openings for meaning.*
> —Mahmoud Darwish

We haven't been in touch much lately, so let me catch you up while I also ask how your eclipse was. Didn't have one? Ah.

Mine was Monday.

Here's a bit of news that I've been facing in myself lately.

How the desire to touch someone may disappear, utterly, for years, then return quite suddenly, in a matter of days or weeks, a haptic emergency.

The movies, full of haptic emergencies. Though these days they mostly cut right to the writhing.

It's 9:48 in the file timestamp here on the page. The eclipse was at about 1:55 where I was. By "eclipse," I mean totality. Totality, then, has a duration.

I should be clear that I was not reading Mahmoud Darwish in protest of the eclipse, though that's kind of a smart-assed thing to say. Perhaps I was reading him in protest of the totality, totality meaning ... I guess some condition we live by that no one has found the right camera angle for just yet.

What else is on my mind? Well, that the flat documentary, that tone, that the flat documentary tone interests me less and less these days. This connects somewhere in my mind with the notion that the essence of certain tactics can be genocidal. Nobody ever talks about tactics.

We wish for rules that spring, somehow, from belief. Though belief itself is conditional on information. Information that changes more quickly than a belief can be formed.

When you or I get angry at the young people, I think it is mostly that we are angry at this condition. Let us cut thirty openings in that, its totality.

It was actually pretty great being raised Unitarian, not to be stuck in, say, the conditions of information the Gautama lived 2500 years ago. And look what happened when he ventured outside the palace, when the conditions of his information changed. Look.

During the eclipse I was standing on karst terrain, next to the bluest water I have seen in the world of my tiny experience, blue due to minerals the water took in as it permeated soft or fractured rock miles away. It trickled and seeped and ran then, into underground torrents, into the welling up, the desire to touch.

I am reading Darwish. I am still reading Darwish by Blue Spring in the Ozarks, in Missouri.

The spring itself, which looks like it goes a few feet down, is actually three hundred feet deep. The ranger says the Statue of Liberty could be immersed completely in its water, and the kid in me imagines her torch going out, making the water briefly boil.

Is that where she's been the past decades of again the war, again the genocide? Is she there with the million dead of Viet Nam? The murdered neighbors of Bosnia? So many. I would be more correct to name them all, but then, there are the tiny, the unknown or unnamed dragged out in a street by some rampant something from miles or centuries away, or what I really mean is someone's son or daughter down my street and what is happening to them in a room where time disappears, I mean each room in each collapsed building on the news, what I mean is my mother dying alone, the book slipping from her grasp during the last breaths, the book undoubtedly a mystery—and forgive me here for my slim experience of unworded suffering—forgive me, but that is what I really mean.

This is for Amira El-Zein, Munir Akash and Carolyn Forché, translators. That just about catches us up I think.

Musée d'Orsay

Like Yosemite, the
   national park, its
      monumental
valley,
     or the Grand Canyon,
   ditto above,
its Kaibab

switchbacks trailed toward
   sunset, colors new
     at each
turn, look!
     that Renoir there
   walking among
these mere

Monets, which are, I
   think, not
     his best,
look! is
     she,
   unattributed
by any placard,

there, in tall boots,
   is she
     the only one
likely
     insecure about her beauty
   where only
the Monets

have reason to be?

MARC VINCENZ

Into the Gilded Age with Marcel Proust
a socio-comedy in five uncertain acts

ONE:
Within a Budding Grove

To acquire the means of happiness
was to plan parties and suppers and picnics;
you'd change clothes five or six times a day.

Then comes the divorce in highlife,
a palatial scandal of dramatic proportions,
a Sensation in New Yoke City; and, of course,

the underlying principle was never discussed.

TWO:
The Captive

What happened in Paris, remains in Paris—
do anything, just don't flaunt it, was the decree;
but the season was coming to an end,

and the powers that be had removed themselves
from Swann's way; who doesn't want to retain custody
of their own godforsaken children?

Social standing can teeter in the blink of an eye.

THREE:

The Fugitive

Yet, the Sensation suddenly found her bearings,
married a robber-baron and built a palace
with faux-Versailles servants and gardens,

with powdered wigs and polished brass buttons,
with canapés on every silver tray and fish eggs
on curved silver spoons that multiplied into infinity.

Either way you look at it, first it jellifies, then it takes form.

FOUR:

The Way

Meanwhile, every evening, the barnyard owl
watched from the cornices—yes, she was tending
to her young: three minor offspring:

one with a deaf ear; another born with stars
in her eyes; the third, a healthy specimen,
was predestined to become The Forever One.

The pinnacle was when her first born was coming out.

FIVE:

And Then, Time Regained

Here was the light in the gilded age, light in general.
It wasn't until they reached San Sebastian, where
her husband originally having hailed from,

that the oysters came into view, and with them too,
the canapés and the duck salad, the foie gras,
and the *gras fumé*; meanwhile, another was born:

she too, with her mother's freckles and curls,

and facing the madding crowd, she became beautiful.

Sentience, an Unperfected Theory

No matter how
hard you might
think—or given

the soft-handed
approach, this
tightrope course—

this, is one of
simple needs, and
subdued caution.

ED FRIEDMAN

from *Midsts*

No, Why?
for Joan La Barbara

Pretty, consonant elements are not for us, Joan.
Imagine we're far enough away, shadows elongated,
from the hundreds of swift new unsold Mustangs, Skylarks,
Furies, and Thunderbirds in La Brea Avenue car lots.
Our "Vowels on the Bass Scale" is danceable, totally fierce,
yet oddly calming in its endless appeal. Figured against light
and always conjuring it, regions and nations under spells
come suddenly awake, open their markets, share wealth.
It's nighttime, spring, and the southwestern toads, (with
bony ridges on their heads either weak or absent)
are trilling—another music near sandy banks and quiet water.
Personally, I was never nocturnal. You?
We go out at dusk but are rarely there overnight.

Flirty Trances

Energy makes the world current. We people, all experts,
stir the roadbed, have our hairs fall out. The flat view—
green sweeps, sand & scrub, muddy canals—forms horizons
stained golden this afternoon, plenty to think about.
Homo sapiens sapiens, our paths intersect and splay.
We push on, stare calmly, camp and cook.
Pick-ups slow down. Stall-outs continue.
You probably know every time we touch each other
irritations mount, skins flush, sentiments shift,
oddly enough, for hours, weeks, lifetimes. Vibrant
and dull meanings take hold—elaborate cultures and unrecordable histories.
One theory, yet unproven, is we dream all we know every night,
and could spend days exchanging knowledge with anybody we want,
and that would be everyone.

More Lines Written in Dark

A big house an old man sitting outside give him a blanket
a good blanket patterned on both sides

I have to leave now but look at him he's like a child you can go now
he has that good blanket

the fragment of a curve suggests an absent arch
the breadth and length of it

wordlessly dimensional the absent

fallen marble the centuries had (illeg.) and there were no (illeg.)

the old man earnestly saying he was satisfied

in the small adjacent building a looping film where the rough eroded
surface of stone completed again and again with full color renderings

what time had impoverished or covered

lifelike the polychrome of Christian images fill space

beneath the arched lintel of a mosque the effort to replace distract from
no invalidate the absent

The Body the Distance Traveled

Morning spills from the bulk of a small house its quiet hour
unyoked to must
shaggy elms raining green benediction

the arbutus with its red fruit a baretrunked palm's spreading crest
dear to the mother of the gods

in dim rooms the few mysteries of light

the leaded body and stunned mind remembering fire

like waking to a front door standing open the panicked survey what's askew

no

the purse still gaping the small box with its small adornments
closed tight it was daylight when you came in

turning on then off the porchlight it must have been wind
so strong anyone could have

the wanting back when you could not speak enough from the bruised body

the ready underworld and its glimpse of anthracite

like bats the names of things irretrievably cling

time to go

your dirty clothes your smoothed skirt did you look ok your shirt that
bore no wrinkle of caring

DAN CAMPION

Little Egypt

Walt Whitman and his younger brother Jeff
  stayed at the American Temperance Hotel
    on Lake and Wabash in 1838.

Henry Thoreau and his young companion Horace
  Mann Jr. stayed at the Metropolitan
    Hotel at Randolph and Wells in 1861.

Such obscure facts flock to me
  like Brando's pigeons, and
    they live in danger too,

as who and what does not,
  considering the principals, the inns,
    the Great Fire, the Days of Rage?

I'd love to see the ledgers Walt and Henry
  signed, the view outside their windows,
    the tables where they dined.

O Margaret Fuller, where did you bed down
  beside the cracked glass lake, and did
    Marcel Duchamp stretch out nearby?

It's just that I'm Chicago-bred,
  rapt for Little Egypt and Sally Rand,
    but transcendental in my civic sense.

The facts roost in their cages,
  watered, fed, mysterious,
    and resolute as feathered fans.

The Arcimboldo Rose

```
                          my hat
             of clover   my
     eyes                  of rye
  my
                    badge
                 of
                 feather
my       belt       of      sky      my
                 mask
     of                  weather
        my
                 beak
                          of
                 plague
           my
                    lap
                             of
                 heather
        my stem
           of sage my
     heart
        of
           river
             my ears
                       of twine
                 my
        boots
           of leather
        my
        lees
        of
           wine
```

TIMONS ESAIAS

Habakkuk on Chaw

For six decades now
the barns have urged me:
Chew Mail Pouch Tobacco
but still
I resist.

Side effects may include
headaches, nausea,
vomiting,
difficulty sleeping,
and a taste for
Dostoevsky.

The key to eternal life
is firm, springy skin
and the right phone
synced to the right software
synced to the latest model
of the perfect car.

Many are spoken to,
but, faithless,
few will listen.
Those who run
neglect to read.

Verily, you have been told.
Mail Pouch tobacco
is the way.

When

When, in Sheol,
Phlegethon's surface
skims over so thick
they break out the saws,
hay, and wagons,
and pack cut blocks
off to ice houses,
against a warmer day.

When I get over
the dream
that was true for
one day only.

When Achilles
faces facts
and says
fuck all this shit
and sails home alive.

When Napoleon listens
to his Master
of Horse;
decides that governing
peacefully
is the best
revenge.

When I burn the letters.

When everyone,
everyone,

finally admits
it was Oswald.
Oswald alone.
Just
Oswald.

WANG PING

Dark Day on Sierra Nevada

The first line is found in the forest
Duff. Under Dark Day Road
Mushrooms run

We call them spirits
Dancing to Esme's songs
We lure them out from underground

Six years of drought
Sierra Mountains flashflood
With mushroom sounds

They jump out of the dark
Red, yellow, lavender, white…in the shape
Of clouds, burning woods with mycelia stars

Line after line
Mound after mound
Who can own the mountain or copyright its children?

The last line leaps into the duff
True soil for wonder, sterile and brown
Ripen with magic

We dance out of the Dark Day Road
Our hearts full
With porcini, blewit, oyster, coral

Never forget the joy, says the mountain
Never forget to play, no matter
How old, grumpy and crippled

Share and taste us, says the mycelia spirit
Never forget where you came from
How wild and happy you used to be

Shoveling Snow

Mid-February, we got the first real snow in the Twin Cities.
It's our duty to shovel, to keep sidewalks clean. People
Moan and hate shoveling. Heavy snow, a few thousand
Shovelings, back pain, shoulder pain, everywhere pain.
I put on my Bluetooth, listening to Gary Snyder's chat
With Elliot. "I studied Keats, Blake, Yeats, Pound, and
Wrote poems, Romantic and academic. Then one day
I burnt them all, renouncing poetry. I walked into the mountains
Paved roads, fixed riverbanks with stones…Then one day
A poem came to me: "Riprap," the first gift from the mountains
And rivers. They told me I can write now, real poems
Because work is no longer work but play."
The audience laughed, and Elliot laughed, asking:
"What do you mean?" I laugh, lifting the heavy snow
Into the sun, letting it fall on trees, garden, each flake
Dancing naked, screeching with joy and gratitude.
Elliot, my old friend from NYC, who loves the carp
I cooked for him, may never understand what it means
That "work is not work but play." He may never know
The taste of working for food and shelter, how the body
And mind can melt into rivers and mountains after endless
Sweating and crying. But Snyder knows the secret:
Chop thousands of wood, shovel tons of snow, fix
Many roads and riverbanks, then you can transform
Your travail into joy, then you can write your "Riprap"
Then you can hear the sound of shovel sliding into snow
The sound of sweating and crying, the sound of the wind
Blowing across grasses, trees and all the things on earth.
That is the sound of cosmos, the sound of poetry.

Two Poets of Inner Mongolia

JIN LINGZI
Translated by Wang Ping

Jin Lingzi (real name, Jian Xinling) a poet and artist, author of nine books of poetry and art, received the 2008 Avantgarde Poetry Award and the Youth Poetry Award from *Poetry Magazine*, as well as the Xu Zhimo and Qu Yuan Prizes. She lives in Chongqing.

Ellipsis

My ellipsis for love can be short or long
If I tell the story, it'd be just adding some noise
The memory is locked in the game of go
It's either black or white; nothing else
Its pain lurks in my laughter
Where tears flow inward
Flooding the lake in my heart
Sometimes, fish and shrimp appear
But I hide them
In the dots
To escape hunters, bullets and nets

This is how I live ... vague, evasive
Sometimes my poetry
Makes some sounds, hollow
Slipping sounds of Go

What Are You Grumpy About?

Why are you grumpy?
You didn't die during the pandemic,
No hunger or cold
You got enough land for chickens
And ducks, even oranges
You can close your eyes,
Look but see nothing
You can open your eyes,
Peep at each other
You ask yourself
What complaints do you really have
You have no answer
Just sit by the mountain, alone
Weeping, in silence

ENKECHADA

Translated by Wang Ping

Enkechada is from Alxa, Inner Mongolia. He writes and publishes poetry in both Mongolian and Chinese. His books of poetry include *Amenwusu, Home of Fast Horses*, and *Saga of Eji Well*. He's the recipient of the Tengeli Poetry Award, the Baby Camel under the Sky Poetry Award, and the Sulongka Award.

The Track of Wind

Wind O wind
I asked you to run to the hitching post
But you came back with the post behind you
The horse ran away, you couldn't catch up

Wind O wind, I asked you to run to my yurt
But you came back carrying it on your back
Because you couldn't find a piece of land
To set my yurt

Wind O wind, I asked you to run in all directions
But you picked up a stone, and came home alone
Because the old home is gone
Even though it shrank to the size of my palm

Wind O wind,
I wish you would run towards me
But you blew through my body
Because I stand naked, I've lost everything!

The Distance of My Home

At dawn, my dreams are torn
Looking through the cracks
I see a painting
Of a camel as big as an elephant
In her eyes
I see my home

At noon I come home from work
The winter sky is broken into pieces
The sunlight flows in from holes
I gaze at the painting on the wall
The camel is in heat, in its eyes
I smell green grass

I look around, footprints everywhere…
The snow-white prints belong to the baby
camels coming home
The prints hotter than the earth belong
to Buddha roaming around the world
The cold prints like ice belong
to the broken painting
The prints darker than my eyes belong
to those who have left home

In the dark, night is approaching
I have a dream in the light of poetry
My dream floats in space—
The horse saddle is still wet
My cold fingers
Stroke the painting on the wall—
The desert in the shape of sand dunes
In the size of my home

The distance of chipping and breaking
Is the distance between countryside and city
The time to heal
Is beyond the dream

TOM WAYMAN

Reading Winter
in memory of Robert Bly

When I try to flatten the book
to hold it open, the binding splits
and in the fissure where pages
separated from other pages, a man
stands on snow

beside the river to watch
overwintering tundra swans
glide, some accompanied by grey-feathered young
while dozens more of the birds
remain stationary, heads under the icy water,
feet paddling to keep
the white triangular rear of their bodies
in air, as their bills feed on
what grows along the shallow bottom.

Miles southward down the valley
only the tops of tombstones are not submerged
in a small white field.

The sky is also a prairie,
a Great Plains
of snow.

HA KIET CHAU

sonnet for my lover circa 1936

the unbeautiful parts of me waited for you
by the river in my mother's yellow áo dài.
i was lotus in silk, and sullen in spring.
you were zephyr blowing the gentlest of flutes.
why does your presence stir up all my wounds?
a breath of air lost between us. unusual. beyond physical.
your face in flashbacks, broken parts fading out:
moon brow, upper lip, freckled star, left cornea—
eventually, the crying ends. we once rode our bikes
up a hill in nha trang, circa 1936, and if you recall
an inkling, confess to me in rem. if fate stood five
feet away, would you recognize it? if destiny brushed
against your arm & disappeared down a black alley,
would you spend lifetimes looking for me?

Semantics & I Love You

After Ba died, language made no sense.
The word *melancholia* sounded like a flower,
not sad enough.
Sheep baaing in the barn, restless, I ponder
the meaning of *I love you* in Vietnamese
and why Ba never said *anh yêu em* to Ma,
not once in their fifty years together.
Someone tell me, is the gate to heaven
close or *closed*? Climbing a hill,
how much closer are we?
Often, my father visits me in dreams,
inside supermarkets, haloed in smoke.
I swear the man in the deli aisle at Foodmaxx is Ba.
At the funeral, I wore blue instead of black
and the breeze that blew that spring
broke the plum tree in our yard,
balls of fruit purpling the dirt roads.
I remember the pigeons,
the feathers, wings, beak and blood.
After Ba died, I wore blue and in the dark,
it gleamed black like I was wearing the night
as incense blew & blew
and the shadow of my mother sobbed.

Fire Aftermath: Inside the Shed

In this room, in this rectangle, the radio
segues from Mandarin to Cantonese pop melodies.
The low, sultriness of Anita Mui's vibrato
relieves tension.

Still, it is difficult to breathe,
smoke continues to fill our lungs.

In the corner bunk, Ma rubs tiger balm
on her ankles, complains of chronic pain.
Ba loathes the smell of mint & menthol,
sighs for the tenth time.

No chair, I am crouched on the floor,
gaze fixed on the glass window—
observing trees swaying, pigeons pecking plums.

Outside it is dusty and pink and beautiful,
and oh god, I am so morose.

Music skipping, radio waves breaking,
Anita's contralto slows to a stop—
trapping us in silence, forcing us to confront
our fears, our losses beneath piles and piles of ash.

I give Ma her Salonpas, Ba his multivitamin.
He sighs again. Yes, I know,
a room without radio is unbearable.

Replacing the batteries, I adjust static, wait
for Anita's rich vocals to flood the spaces
between us, sweeping the terrible silence
out the door.

AMY DE ROUVRAY

Apartment Building in Paris

Do you still paint?
She asked as we rode the elevator to the second floor.

I didn't recall ever painting.
Her husband had been an artist,
but a car accident landed him in a wheelchair.
They met at the Hotel Lutetia, where survivors were cared for
after concentration camps.
Typically, I preferred to ride the elevator alone.
My eyes fled to the walls
of our tight compartment, to the words and sketches
carved in wood, most of them obscene.

You had such talent with colors.

At the back of the apartment, my room had white carpet
and Laura Ashley prints.
Rabbit-shaped bookends held up school textbooks,
a porcelain doll rested on a shelf,
a crown of dried flowers, a framed photo of the dog.
There were no paintbrushes in paint-stained glasses,
no squeeze bottles oozing acrylic.
A sheltered space among carefully collected items,
Easter chocolates untouched, and a closet door held shut.

Her husband died.
I saw through the front door into their apartment,
past the mezuzah that hung underneath the doorbell,
an explosion of orange and red, heavy silk drapes, and Persian rugs.

Did I paint?
The possibility of color splattered on white carpet,
canvas pinned onto walls, brushes stacked, light pouring in.
She nodded, the elevator doors sliding shut behind her,
as I continued to the fourth floor.

Name It

My father marched ahead across the curved bridge,
pointing at yellow flowers budding in a field of grass.
    Crocus (not daffodil).
We stopped by a tree of frail pink and white blossoms,
grasping their branches in the wind.
    Prunus (not cherry).
A shrub settled along the South wall of the house,
warming its purple blooms in the sun.
    Ceanothus (not lilac).

Stroll, not run. Stand, not roll in the grass. Listen, not speak.

Gripping his walking stick like a scepter,
he indicated the features of buds, bark, leaves,
how they'd turn in the fall.
The maple, now a bright green, would glow red and gold.

Facing me, he waited, gaze fixed
as if the chisel of his mind could carve onto my brain,
    as if I were rock.

A name failed to reach my lips—tilia, platanus, salvia.
The flavor of spring in my gut turned to coal.

Years later, I hold a hand smaller than mine and follow my child
down a forest path.
We notice the dew resting on young leaves,
observe a trunk, its wound healing where there once was a branch.
A feeling I don't name fills my heart.

BROOK J. SADLER

The Mathematics of Love

Multiplication is a form of addition,
only faster. Fornication is a form of
love, plus disaster.
          Monogamy adds one
to one, but the whole is more than the sum
of the parts.
          Yet, when two lovers divide,
their hearts are not wholes, but mere fractions.

Separation unbalances balanced equations.

Numerical values can be rounded up
or down. Love's accounting is less precise,
but more exacting.
          Jealousy, when estimated,
counts as overreacting. And betrayal plots
an asymptotic curve:
          Trust, once lost,
can be infinitely approached, but never reached.
Love exists on only one side of the breach.

From the Dream Awakened

I dreamt I wore my watch upside down,
and the date scrolled backward from thirty-one.
I lived my life in reverse, already knowing what I'd sown—
before, by a logic perverse, it had even been done.

I dreamt I loved all the wrong people,
loved them all so passionately and well
that I fooled myself, and I was a fool,
and I felt my life was a happy sequel

to a story I knew but could not tell.
I dreamt I danced when I should have cried.
I dreamt I rhymed when I should have lied.
I dreamt my body was a toll

paid every day, handed out like seed
to birds, a fee given to the universe
for the right to be. I dreamt I took a side
and took the other side, too, out of greed.

I dreamt it could have been worse.
It could have been that colors were sounds,
that powder blue was way too loud,
and all the hues of dawn were wounds,

and sunset an unbearable opera.
But then, like a snow-globe up-turned,
I dreamt I woke to gently-falling drama.
All was soft and white and easily learned.

I dreamt there was no truth I did not know,
and all the roads taken and not-taken converged,
like tributaries in the sea. Thus on the verge
of waking, I shivered once and was sure which way to go.

MARY CISPER

Indigo Bunting

How, on Charlie's porch,
a diving pelican
will stop your

thought

before you know it
to check if there's a fish

(a swallow?)

and weather,
a tattered social excuse
or experience of

sublimity

if appearance
(more sparrow
than goldfinch?)

call forwards

a bridge
between
islands.

Scrap on Which is Written, peony

As *Pleiadian* is to *Capacious*,
font is to typeface a little arial—

(Whitehead writing of God:
"It is the function of actuality to characterize the creativity")

In other words, two pennies:
Lincoln is dead, Lincoln is alive

and if coinage slips into illegible sparrows in trees,
try grounding for a while

"spread more mulch"
"move the devil's trumpet"

while skinks undermine the rock border
but no, they're whiptails.

An *excess* of hummingbirds   or not an excess
trips on symbolic language:

is this your stomach or your belly,
do you care about beauty queens.

        A scrap tugs at the future:
is it a leaf   or a horse galloping—

Fanfiction: Enchanted

In dreams begin responsibilities
—Delmore Schwartz

A cabin in the unincorporated county is no fairytale cottage
but there are plenty of woodland creatures.
Snake season starts in three weeks.

Just now I feel like Giselle because two mice are frolicking
on the floorboard of my car.

To be a waif and not a wife. To have a tale
and not a life.

You know the frog that's being slowly …
That's not water: it's responsibility. A protean medium
which can appear almost anywhere.

It freezes me in place
when I just want to let go, it turns my libido
to wet cardboard.

Responsibility doesn't begin in dreams
it begins in landlord/tenant dialectics, in the interest-bearing loan.

Dreams are gracefully extinguished by responsibility
unless they flame out, doused in all that good behavior.

I feel bad for Patrick Dempsey—
he'd rather be a full-time race car driver than a movie star.

It must be terrible to be good at something
so lucrative you can never quit.

It must be awfully expensive to insure your hair.
To be continually cast as a doctor or lawyer
when all you ever wanted to be was Evel
Knievel.

I dream of doing something so irresponsible
I can't even write it down, can't say it out loud.

Let me tell it to you in chipmunk-squeak, in mime.
Let me sing and dance it, let me act it all out.
Sit back, relax—this could take a little time.

ZIGGY EDWARDS

Resting Place

I wouldn't want to inflict the truth on anyone
if I'm not completely sure
but certainty is a trap

Comfort keeps me still
lying still in a beautiful field
with a burning horizon

but what's not to love
about lying still in a beautiful field?

I hope my beautiful field is not destroyed
but I think it probably will be destroyed

Then lying still will not bring comfort anymore
and I'll run in one direction or another
into some trap or another

If certainty doesn't drive the soldier,
is it revenge for the corpse in a burning field?

MARK PAWLAK

True North Notebook Pages

Wanted: Fish processing technicians, True North Maine.

Rt. 1 North of Whiting

Weathered board nailed to utility pole:
hand lettered, advertising, "Fresh Air."

Roadside signage: "Shore Better Than Work."

Roadside signage: "All Things Dirt and Concrete."

*

Wilson's Beach Pier

Humpbacks off-shore in channel:
breach, spout;
flukes in air, deep dive.

Whale-watch boats swarm.

*

Lubec

Dusk: wharf hushed.
Boats at anchor in harbor
bows facing outgoing tide.

A door, heard but not seen, slams shut;
heard but not seen,
tires crunching gravel;

mewling gulls, clank of rigging;
Johnson Bay:
riffles on silvered glass.

*

Lexicon:

Dimpled pewter woven with silver ribbons …

Crinkled foil, strewn glitter, washboard ridges …

Flinty, frothy, scudding …

Slate, gunmetal, graphite, ash …

*

Herring Cove

They carry canvas folding chairs
up and over the steep berm,
open them on coarse sand.

Rocky bluffs bookend cove.
Two net-draped weirs,
two curled question marks.

Where surf meets pebbly strand,
a mother stands guard,
children chase retreating waves.

White smudge on horizon,
smoke curls trailing:
container ship? Island ferry?

Incoming tide nibbles weir poles;
surf shuffles, reshuffles its cards
shoreline creeps.

On coarse sand, two seated figures:
their lengthening shadows.
They just might stay put forever.

*

Contraband

Cantharellus cibarius

"There'll be mosquitos," she says.
      "Yes, I know"
"And maybe black flies."
      "Maybe black flies."
"And poison ivy, too."
      "Un-huh,"
"And cars on that narrow dirt road."
      "I'll be careful."
"There isn't room enough for two to pass."
      "I'll be careful.
"There's no shoulder."
      "I'll be careful."
"Won't the woods be mucky?"
      "Spongy, not mucky."
"Wet, squishy moss?"
      "Yes, that's ideal."
"You know you can't bring them back."
      "You mean across the border?"
"Remember the seashells … the customs guy?"
      "He only gave us a scolding."
"But they'll confiscate them."
      "If they find them."

"You like taking chances."
      "I'm not smuggling cocaine."
"You like taking chances."
      "I've waited all year for this."
"Don't forget the bug spray."

*

Magritte Canvas

Gray metal roof peak
fogbound bay beyond
island hill tops
floating untethered.

*

Bayview

Fir-topped islands
girdled in fog:
their upside down
saw-tooth reflections!

*

Quilt

Bolt of cotton batting
slowly unfolding,
slowly folding back up.

*

O, Canada!

> *I drew a map....*
> —Joni Mitchell, "A Case of You"

Out early. International Bridge across narrows:
Camp-o-bello. Lubec Channel ferry crossing:
leeward, The Sow ; starboard, Indian Island.
Deer Island head landing:
rocky strand, tires crunching stone.
Narrow, patched, roller coaster two-lane:
Doctors Cove, Chocolate Cove, Hibernia Cove,
Lords Cove, Leonardville, Northeast Harbor,
Fish Harbor, Lambertville, Stuart Town pier.
Coastal Transport Ferry's horn blast.
Fundy Bay "notch" to Letete, Letang.
North, St. George; West, St. John; East, St. Stepehen.
"O Canada!" St. Andrews by the Sea.
King Street, Queen Street, Prince of Wales Street;
Windsor House, Char & Chowder, Island Quest Marine,
Boutique Le Baleine—"O Canada!"

*

Headlines on facing pages of *Quoddy Tides*:
"Pirates to Set Sail"
"Salmon to Be Served"

* * *

poems from T O D A Y

9.8

light grey whiteness of fog against invisible ridge two sparrows landing by
   seeds on table beside fence

things seen for what they are part in one's life pictured presents response
   to present made present act

breathing in eyes opening motion of shadowed green leaves on branch in
   window above yellow and blue bed

diagonal white edge of fog against shoulder of ridge lines of waves
   breaking to the left across channel

9.9

light grey whiteness of fog against invisible ridge sparrow landing beside
   seeds on table next to fence

front figures weather the stone made to look like a line the person again
   part head arms range of hills

breathing in breathing out eyes opening motionless black leaves on
   branch in window yellow and blue bed

grey white fog against top of shoulder of ridge sound of waves breaking
   on sand to the right of channel

9.10

light grey whiteness of fog against top of shadowed ridge two towhees
    beside seeds on table below fence

colors in landscape five fifty seventy days of sketches more finished relate
    in way back to during time

breathing in breathing out eyes opening shadowed green leaves on
    branches in window yellow and blue bed

grey whiteness of fog against top of shoulder of ridge line of wave
    breaking to the left across channel

9.11

blinding white circle of sun in cloudless blue sky above ridge 3 sparrows
    by seeds on table below fence

follow thought speaking of language something spoken more than first
    listen to the window falling steps

breathing out eyes closed opening motion of shadowed green leaves in
    window next to yellow and blue bed

blinding whiteness of sun coming up above shoulder of ridge sunlit waves
    breaking into mouth of channel

9.12

light grey whiteness of fog against invisible ridge two sparrows landing by
    seeds on table beside fence

phenomenon of perception to the end of appearance other than horizon
    far from in fact figure before one

breathing in breathing out eyes opening blue jay landing on branch in
    window beside yellow and blue bed

grey whiteness of fog against invisible shoulder of ridge sound of wave
    breaking on sand beside channel

MARK DUCHARME

The Crisis

The crisis is inside us
What you do is what you believe
Test parts of worlds gone by
Nobody's speaking

    The crises are outside us
    Idle tender
    Everybody's listening
    Or else jerking off

When I am *in* the poem
A thwarted ideal
Left to win
In vital effigies

    Where all is dross
    Tender & brutal
    Give me, friends, the energy I need
    To survive one more day

Elegy

Shed the norm in your purgatorio
Sleek as January trumpets
The ones held in

Norm the pour in your mediated grimace
Migrate yourself & see how it feels
If the wind trembles at the tips of a hummingbird's wings

If the sky's color's palpable as the lips of bleeding children
Swallow your tongue, your voice
Swallow all the shit in silly con with a voice no longer telling

Don't tell
Don't let yourself be told
Don't fire. Look the other way & moan

Listless as penitents in Pensacola
Tuneless as loiterers in Tuscaloosa
Foundered as news anchors in Ashtabula

Look it in the eyes
Nobody home
This night was made for fleeing

BRUCE BEASLEY

Sacrosanctions

It would bleed you out of yourself,

reads the Latin inscription—
in ink made from nails
boiled in vinegar—purge

you of your self-possession
& its companion self-detesting.

Ego-omnium-et-nihil.

Its incipient letters burnished
in gold leaf and cinnabar, the elixir's
recipe stands re-
revealed,
tight-scrolled in a clay jar
till Danube floods crushed open its cave's
millennium-long niche of hiding.

It's been prepared today

particularly for you:
wormwood, wine, bitterroot, cloves,
rue. Think of all your gotten
lauds: prizes, laureates, applauses
that don't end. Dwell on those
that scarcely begin,
then seal your eyes & slurp
slowly
slowly from the vial.

Oboe
adagios and cello
pizzicatos
will quicken the tempo
of your diminuendo.

Is *I* still
your first word
when you wake? Here,

it wouldn't hurt to take
a few deep drafts more.

ADAM ZDRODOWSKI

Leiden, House by Oude Vest
for Urszula

A house by the canal will do
een huis aan de gracht, for now
as there's nothing else but now
we're growing older, forever and for now.

Een huis aan de gracht, for now
is a projection of our fancy ten years into the future.
Yet we're growing older, forever and for now.
Will houses and canals stand and flow forever still?

A projection of our fancy ten years into the future,
A safe haven, a place of stone, glass and wood.
Will houses and canals stand and flow forever still?
Stuck between water and sky, we're made of dreams and stars.

With no safe haven, a place of stone, glass and wood
no insurance and low credit score
stuck between water and sky, we're made of dreams and stars.
We are scrabble players, readers of Bishop, students of Blake

with no insurance and low credit score.
When the sun is out, we surf the web and rage.
We are scrabble players, enamoured of Dylan Thomas
shopping for shadows, driftwood and clouds.

When the sun is out, we surf the web and shop.
I was sold a map of the sky, updated and revised.
shopping for shadows, driftwood and clouds
I came upon a guide to the underworld, second edition, unabridged.

I was given a map of the sky, re-revised and updated
for now, as there's nothing else but now and
a guide to the underworld, second edition, unabridged.
It's entitled *A House by the Canal*.

in our latitudes

down in the park a boy
is weeping over the sunset
he failed to see, as the night beyond
the park grows dark and
darker still. Don't cry, little boy
there will be other lost sunsets
as the horizon draws nigh, and
new roads, straight and narrow
and dazzling days beyond count, unmarked
in the ledger of the itinerant
calendar salesman. Hush
little boy: the day lies in wait
the night is dark, the world
is still, right here, down in the park

REBECCA LILLY

Night Pond

Knock on a blindman's bluff, and psychological laws dictate that it opens: lodestars of make-believe tumble out, a twilight of idols (gnomish homunculi from the burial holes of my desires). I'm always looking for the real without the lie, but it's hard to discern much at night without moonlight; floorboards pitch to forge shadows as I pace the room back and forth, giving image to my thoughts. The silence is shatterproof as my mind lights candles for its practice of writing the invisible. But can I analyze my life, or identify truth, with the windows icing in my living room? *By directing your obsessions to the outside*, some voice in me answers. So I leave by the backdoor for the forest, dusting life in the understory, with wind as my accompaniment, a blindman's bluff. And yet, in putting on a blindfold to feel my way through the woods, my existence never doubts itself. As I draft poems on its night-crossed insignia, the homunculi of my desires are owl calls from the conifers hedging a pond. Another rendering of blindman's bluff, it's how the poem requests you stay the night with us.

JOEL DAILY

The Chihuahua Doesn't Bite

While picnicking beneath an all-terrain vehicle
A breeze delivers the distinct aroma of burnt celebrity
Deforestation or defenestration?
Pyro or active blogger?

In the 9 to 5 trenches nobody's imperfect
Discourse off course
Do you allow enhanced interrogation techniques on the first date?
Day to day it's hand to footlong

Meanwhile @ dunch Subject ingests Amarillo
Who peddles longevity from the trunk of a '67 Camaro?
Engorged aliens have landed
They are not impressed

Poetry's Awful Secret
for Chris Toll

All gone cattywampus
Algorithms awry
Popeye pops his 17th can of spinach
A painfully green brontosaurus treads water nearby

A confusion of quarks
"Hi! My name's Joel   I enjoy throwing food away"
High performance to comfy casual
Wad on Bloor

Intersections fail to intersect
Is why Beijing doubles down
Trend-responsive,
The sun tossing cookies over the yardarm

Runs primarily concurrently first one way then the other
A Compensated Spokesperson I am not
Jesus steps from a UFO in Bug Splat, Arkansas
Pivotal to the transformation

JOSEPH NOBLE

from Kandinsky Improvisations

7. *Watercolor after Bild mit weissem Rand (Painting with White Border)* 1915

a landscape riding through
itself

a landscape riding through
after itself

a bridge or a road
sand dialogue

drum reach
iris circling hawkweed

diastole systole
blood games with dice eyes

sing itch climbs
inch after itself

skin thrumming
see saw to said

37. *Ins Dunkel (Into the Dark)*, May 1928

in the dark, in the eye,
in the steps: the hand against air.
in the shoulders: another hand.
in the room, in the invented direction,
in the book left on the bus:
a note written only in vowels
a wall being touched
a swallow feeling its eye.
in the location left to its own devices:
skins up against each other.
in the gesture carving icons at the fingernail,
in the shadow swallowing its birds:
a corner, a moth, a neck.
in the joke's medicine:
a stone long in the tooth
a dog neither hide nor hair.

ANTHONY SEIDMAN

Towards a Graphology of Death

Not a leap into crypto-virology,
not a lecture from the glossary of phantom bacterium,
not even a new cephalopod discovered
in the abyssopelagic zone;

to seek
the scripture beneath DNA,
to apprehend
the alphabet of dissolution,
the palimpsest of extinctions;

to translate
the vowel and its palindrome
inside platelets,
the terminal semiotics
be it semaphore
or growling,
an echo since birth inside
encephalic twilight;

therefore,
death's scripture
scrawls liquid architecture,
an altar of smoke,
nightmarish lactation;

the dying one
bereft of decoding death's handwriting,
that obscure codex,
whose titular etymology
writhes arachnid, consisting
of molted exoskeletons;

the moribund
is a plinth supporting no statue,
a crumbling caryatid,
no wiser than the last phrenologist;
his death-gnosis,
a cenotaph erected in drought.

I Call Your Name

Having missed our appointment,
I send you my double
whom you won't recognize.

Now I await you
where a black bull disembowels
horses, then dons a top-hat,

at the center of the center where
each evening

I exhale a hole through which
the carmine of your surname
glistens the pediments and vectors

from some extinct alphabet.

WILLIAM VIRGIL DAVIS

Restorer

She sits for hours staring at a single spot,
wondering how she will ever be able to get
it right, to make her work as original as
the original. The afternoon light creeps
up behind her, putting her hand in shadow.
There is just enough light left to see as he
must have seen, when he asked this girl
from down the street to change her clothes
and take the pose she sees her in. And she
wonders about that, too, whether that young
woman thought much about it, after all: what
she might be, years later, as she stood and
stared into the distance behind his left ear
and heard, instead of the bustle in the street
outside, a distant music coming back to her
quite surprisingly from somewhere in her
early childhood, her mother singing low,
almost under her breath, while she, still a
child, sat dreaming about the life she longed
and hoped for, in the nearby village—not
knowing how improbable, really, that would
be. What was it had drawn her here, to this
room, to sit there and stare at that one small
spec of blue, at that other young woman,
who had been dead for two hundred years?

KAMI ENZIE

Matchbox Mattress

It arrived while we were away. Left in front
of the door to our apartment, it was not stolen.
It did not catch fire, as it occasionally would.

I was shy about bringing it in. When I turned
from the elevator and saw the box standing
there like a man, I looked at the colorful carpet.

"No way am I paying for some enormous
bedframe with strike-pads on it of phosphorus,
binder, and powdered glass," you said jokingly

to our new friends at the store, an attractive
young couple who had the same mattress.
"Rule #1. Buy a special airbed for nights

your mattress doesn't want to sleep with you.
Rule #2. Find a private spot for resentments
that don't evaporate in a day, a part of the bed

your partner won't want to see. Corollary to #2:
There will be fights you will need him to recognize
your money and disappointment as yours alone."

Those were the laws Jeremy and Ryan laid
before leaving, ahead of us in line.
It was not long before clothes turned black

and I painted head and neck alizarin red.
Soon we couldn't find sticks to rub, nor fuel
in the belongings we learned to love instead.

Steam and Steam

Hands over knees, pulled hooves on chair.
Skinny as dogs, tummies as tight. You leave.
We work in the city that gets paid each day.
Then at home change clothes before dinner.
Bite in legs, fingers on bones. Habanero,
garlic, carrot, onion. To get to another life
through another's mouth, the wings
prepare themselves for the body.

C PIRLOUL-BROSHI

The Little Desk

Doppelgängerangel of 20yearme's *Faces*
Of My Future Lovers—triangular shard to
My embrace perfectly
Shaped so 4 fingers ('tween-
Aged soulsisters splayed cross
Funky'60ssofa legs flung over its
Back knees peaked ankles slack) loungeround You while
Ventral thumb basetopad marries the
Many to Onemass (asin aerial sight
Surfs soften cliffcutsedimentaries : Your
Chistley retractioncornicecrazycresting remainders) no
Matter how
You I rotate (chunk with one tiny absent
Twig turnedcave) Your fit's fine
To my hand. Yours

A small life—
A single cypress-like's
Centrifuged millennia—
Surface morphed pearly to shrapnel and
Acne pock by latitudinal
Crack division cohering in crevasse
Of finest silk fibrillae warp—Phloem pre-
Antiquity what
Have you seen what
Fed—formed—beat—bore Your
Arch desire and defeat

Here
Erratica scars shaft a woof
To hold You together—Here—
Your compression's polish glows failed

Rubylift diminished hemoglobin livid for air — — — Will
Torque You teach accomplish? Channel
Absorption and transmutation of horrors only
Cheapened by talk —fossilsoul—

— Speak

The Little Desk

6 small2large1"gold" binder clips
Squeezed to riot in squat fake pewter
Cylinder next its lid of fake pewter
Rimming a plastic film porthole—half
Slid off a smooth round palewood finger
(Memory: raincoming cool penetrates
As we munch sandwich seated on fallen
Log last fall I pick up the smooth sided
Shorn to sharptip stick)—length
And shape of my 7th rib (armor shielding
Discernment and taste truncates Breath's
Upper reach while peaking its billow of
Draw) but torn in half lengthwise so the
Concave back of its convex curve reveals
Its compact rivers streamingstraight in
Dense grain—laid on a snapped foot
Of juniperfinger—minifractal component
Of its whole—its gruffbark long lost meso
Derm rolled round cracks and tiny darkeyed
Wounds left by aborted twigs once trans
Ported nutrients now dehydrated to
Chollagray VanGoghArles fishing nets
With festerwide gapes revealing a spindle of
Vertical determination accrued by daily
Yearly sunray attunement to core this
Pillar a brittle memory of limber stormsurfer

NEIL SHEPARD

Lucky Stars

*

Something tells me I'll need a star-chart,
charging station, and phosphorescent bridge
to get there if I'm honest about approaching
poetry. And maybe I'll need an omni-
directional signal and a forecast
free of obfuscation. Here's my first
quandary: How one luminous choice limits
another. How the metaphor of gravediggers
buries the metaphor of caretakers; how the image
of flowering catalpa perfumes the cesspool
alongside the trees; how the dumpster seagull
leads ineluctably to its seacoast double;
how one mention of Zen sends ascension
to hell; how poetic compression inhabits
a different economy than the syntax
of Jamesian qualifiers and absolute
constructions in the secret gardens
of the sixteenth arrondissement!
So I stop at the end of a line and refuse
the maneuver that will make a difference.
And two, I'm immediately groggy
in the presence of poetry, meaning
I'm constantly brewing pots of pizzazz
or else – or else, risk the death of the buzz,
the slip of propulsive energies that came
to me as charged language,
that keeps this thing flying toward the stars.
At some point, the fuel, the juice, runs out,
the rocket-stages detach and fall away,
and the lonely nose of this vehicle and tenor
better be loosed from gravity by then or else –

or else, it incinerates, disappears without a trace –
unless a god, a muse, a signal from a dithyrambic
station somewhere in the Olympic peninsula
tracks the poem as it plummets, while I lie
down among the columbines
poking up beside receding glaciers
and wait till dark to count my lucky stars.

1968 Ghosts

Those were the days after I'd cracked up in boot camp,
and I was living in a hotel room on Amsterdam Avenue
with a cot, a hotplate, a mini-fridge, and a floor lamp—
King and Bobby were murdered, but, reader, you knew.

I was living in a hotel room on Amsterdam Avenue—
the bathroom was down the hall, and it was always damp;
King and Bobby were murdered, but, reader, you knew.
I was assigned a psychiatrist: she was my Vietnam off-ramp.

The bathroom was down the hall, and it was always damp
from the hookers who worked there, after taking showers.
I was assigned a psychiatrist, who was my Vietnam off-ramp.
One hooker offered a freebie, but I couldn't get it up for her.

The hookers who worked there monopolized the shower.
I was on so much Thorazine, one nicknamed me *the zombie*—
another offered me a freebie, but I couldn't get it up for her.
I had been torn between hating the war and serving my country.

I was on so much Thorazine, I was nicknamed *the zombie*.
Those were the days after I'd cracked up in boot camp.
I was torn between hating the war and serving my country.
My room had a cot, a hotplate, mini-fridge, and floor lamp.

KEVIN DUCEY

Disposable Box

No words from my grandmother.
My mother's laughter: Erin go bragh.
All that American tin pan alley: The
eyes are smiling at the joke.

                        That summer's
dark windowless kitchen, Formica-top
table. Remember climbing the metal frame
chairs and finding a small box of cereal.

Each kid gets their own box in this country.
You cut your carton of sugar flakes open.
Tear into the face of the Tiger, the Elves,
or insipid Leprechaun. Butter knife
leaves ragged edge cardboard and wax paper.

Peel it all aside and pour in the milk, as if
you're swamping a boat. Wait for word
to go to hospital and then funeral.

Decades later, gene tracing tells me
grandad kept a second family up in
Montreal, and there's a story
with no words.
                But what magic
we owned then—to change
one thing to another with a knife.

JOHN CROSS

Paper Airplane

If there really are infinite numbers of universes
hidden in plain sight, I could be
raising a hand in greeting
& later that afternoon, it's a sad so long.
Or elsewhere, buoyantly lingering over the skeletons
of creatures who swam a clear ocean, I juxtapose
unrelated things to create weird new meanings
while later that evening, rain soaked & stepped on,
I stoop over with the poor posture of a bitter man.
Wherever I am, should I catch up with myself,
I hope I'm living as harmlessly as I can,
carefully preserving the threads that anchor us
to all the places we've been, but now it seems
each time I turn a corner
I'm right back where I was.

Today's sky through our kitchen window

is friends gone
    distant snow

is here one skeleton has been propped up since
   phrases started to vanish along the edge

 is listen
my head goes its own way
  one ear to the cold morning the other
   to memories of radiators & pharmacies
    like the earth's face bumping into things

 listen
my head goes its own way
   enamored by the circle it makes
    longing to be no more alone
     than the rest of us

JOEL CHACE

Against Which

Unclenched fist. Hand that touches, then
paints, a cave's ceiling. Hand that
holds a pen. Hand that washes
the second step. *Not long ago,*
I had three suns, now the
two best have set. Hand that
becomes a paten—on it, her
eyes. *If only my third sun*
would follow, I should feel happier
in the dark. Hand, now transformed,
that so gently pushes every timid
wanderer through the door to the
        labyrinth.

Unclenched fists. Hands that fling open
those round gates of the blue
morning stars. Hands that hang on
the way a lute with its
green ribbon, which will, fluttering strings,
create a sighing song. *People make*
us lonelier by reminding us of
God. Hands that press and smooth
a notebook page. *There's nothing in*
there that wouldn't make us weep.
Hands that remove an empty paten
from its shelf. *And the angels*
Cut off their wings and every
Morning return to earth.

Immense shift, into which she changes
prior to sundowning, to prayer. Prior
to prior. *If there were only*
a way to stop this. In this
array, she's immoveable as that
saint, heavy as the moon. She,
of course imagines death: no longer
can she burn, but a saber
through the throat might do it.
Where is faith? *No one can*
be an atheist who does not
know all things. Only God is
an atheist. The devil is the
greatest believer, and he has his
reasons. If someone comes, right now,
to her door, she'll ask, *Have*
you come to play me beautiful,
                useless music?

Immense shift—child sees its sheared
curls flutter down beyond mother's slippered
feet and into fireplace flames. Instant
nothingness. Instant grief. *He'd come to
the Laboratory, seen several friends, talked
cheerfully.* So the child now places
all faith in its imperishable, large
iron key. Soon, rusting begins, and
the most bitter tears of life.
*Then, alone, he died, close to
his desk, between the maps and
fossils. Absurd. Or wonderful.* In that
deep linen drawer, they find their
child, who says it's lying in
the grave. Snow falls into waves.
Snow falls into snow. Truth into
truth. *Truth does not break anything.*
The quick. The maimed. The dead.
          The dying.

LOGAN FRY

Charm

The limp grin went undaunted, dauntless, along
Now ripped acerbic from a placid hint toward lure's ignition,

A cork put in mention. Went with the cureless. Jestered.
Instinct's trickle. Pissed in the eclipse. In lead I lie bathed.

Abashed and embittered,
Sent with intent, languid.

Rainfall's bent tickles the bricks rotten.
There isn't a lament pneumatic enough.

To whip the rent particles back into the appearance of being.
Nor is apparition a spackled lather of regret's concupiscence.

Tame me in its mirror of finish.
Hand over the polishing cloth.

Content Is a Glimpse

Leave it with the weather: Mustard
And a leash, and the will to perish, and
An apricot that's mush on its resting edge.
Poise has no one to thank nor to beg of.

But I can't get the configuration settled.
It's not that character is featureless, it's that
One can grasp a sturdiness in some
That persists broadly. Take the cow path

Of amity, I await, with a worn knife and
Your likeness. Charm sown in that cleft
Like a fetish. Measly, the still germ
Of this wind, a wish, a pittance of lingering.

www.ingramcontent.com/pod-product-compliance
Lightning Source LLC
Chambersburg PA
CBHW020902090426
42736CB00008B/472

* 9 7 8 1 9 6 8 4 2 2 0 7 3 *